LEADER**SHIP**WRECKED

Charting a New Course for Leadership

DEDICATION

I dedicate this book to the following bright lights in my life:

To R.G. for sharing and caring and being open to continuing our growth journey together. I learn from you every time we interact, and I can't thank you enough.

BTW: R.G. also designed the beautiful cover for this book and I'm just in love with it!

To J.B.H. for truly inspiring me every day, even though we don't talk daily. Your core goodness makes me strive to be a better person so that I'm worthy of your friendship. Your continued support and feedback are priceless.

To J.M.H. for being there for me no matter what or when, no matter how much she has on her own plate, or how ridiculous I'm being. She's my biggest fan and I will continue to work hard to earn her love and support.

To M.B.F. for showing me what true strength and perseverance looks like, and for doing so with grace, positivity, and love.

And last but most certainly not least, to my husband. He puts up with all my imperfections and weirdness and supports my work even when he doesn't get it. He is the perfect partner for me on this journey we call life, and I am so blessed.

A NOTE FROM THE AUTHOR:

Leadership is different today than it was a decade ago. Heck, it's different than it was 5 years ago – even 2 years ago! And if we really want to continue to be impactful leaders, we have to adapt our leadership style and approach our service in an ever-changing manner.

Be aware, it's hard work. Really hard work.

But you've taken the first step by grabbing a resource to help you.

I can almost promise you that there are some ideas in this book that are going to be difficult for you to wrap your mind around. That's OK. Don't stop reading just because a concept in that chapter is too 'out there' for you right now. It might be helpful later once it's completely sunk in.

It's my true hope that this book will inspire you and help you on your journey of leadership transformation, but if it does nothing but get you to think about your leadership approach a bit differently than you did in the past, then I'll take that as a win!

Mindy McCorkle

The names of the people referenced in this book have been changed to protect their privacy, but the stories are REAL!

CHAPTER 1:
YESTERDAY'S LEADERSHIP

Traditional Leadership

When most people think of traditional leadership, they think of words like: Example, inspiration, honesty, vision, motivation, and influence.

And those are all applicable.

Who is someone you perceive to be a great leader?

When I ask that question in seminars and workshops, I get answers like Oprah Winfrey, Martin Luther King, Maya Angelou, Steve Jobs, Richard Branson, mothers, fathers, ministers, etc. The list goes on and on.

Who is someone YOU see as a great leader?

Now think about the reason, or reasons, that you believe that person is a great leader.

We all have our own ideas about what it means to be a great leader. It may be because of something he or she has accomplished. It could be something specific they've done or positive changes they've forged in a particular arena.

But chances are it has something to do with something they've done for someone else. Their contribution to the greater good, the way they've mentored others, or the inspiration they provide to those around them.

In your list of reasons, you probably see evidence of a leader being someone who is willing to sacrifice their own interests for the good of others.

The Fundamentals of Leadership

Chances are, you bought this book because you know traditional leadership is no longer working – it's wrecked. And you know we must transform our leadership approach to be effective in the future. And I applaud you!

And we'll get there, I promise.

But first, we need to lay down the fundamentals.

Leadership must be earned. You can't buy it, or have it assigned to you. It has to be developed over time. It cannot be given to you. Or appointed.

The top positions in the organizations are not necessarily the leaders of the organization. Leadership has absolutely nothing to do with position, or role. And in today's business world, it is no longer acceptable to rely on our position to identify us as a leader. We cannot think of ourselves as leaders simply because we're in a 'leadership' position.

True leaders are not figureheads. They are the ones in our midst that understand that the strength of an organization or a collective group comes from the people within, not from their own abilities or skills. They know that what they do and the decisions they make are about others, not themselves. And they know the best proof of true leadership is not the leader's personal success but the success of those influenced by that leader.

We have to *choose to lead*.

And once we make that choice, we have to work at it!

You may have made a conscious decision to lead at some point in your adult life.

Some of us just woke up one day and realized that others were following us and that made us choose to continue to lead.

You don't have to have direct reports, or supervise others, in order to lead in your workplace. Because it's not about position or responsibility, you can be seen as a leader in your organization no matter your role. But you have to *choose to lead.* (Tired of hearing that yet?)

It's that ability to lead regardless of position or role that sets the true leader apart from the rest. These true leaders want to help others, even if it means extreme inconvenience for themselves.

Traditional leadership is about influence: the art of getting others to do something that needs to be done because they want to do it. And there are only two ways to influence human behavior: manipulation or inspiration. Managers manipulate. Leaders inspire.

And while we're on the subject of managers versus leaders....

Leadership is NOT management.

Some people use the terms management and leadership interchangeably. That's inaccurate, in my opinion. They are not the same thing. Leadership and management are both important roles, but they are not the same thing at all.

As crazy as our workplace can be these days, unfortunately we often resort to management when leadership is called for.

If you're a manager, you're focused on systems, processes, planning, budgeting, organizing, staffing, and best practices. Problem-solving is the core of being a manager. Managers are charged with making sure front-line workers know *how* to do the tasks they are assigned.

Management is 'this is what I think' and leadership is 'what do you think?' Management follows the rules; leadership reinvents the rules. Management is a title; leadership is a choice.

Take the Chick-fil-A® sandwich. New associates working in the kitchen are instructed on how to make this popular sandwich.

As a manager, you will likely approach the task of teaching how to assemble this sandwich similar to this:

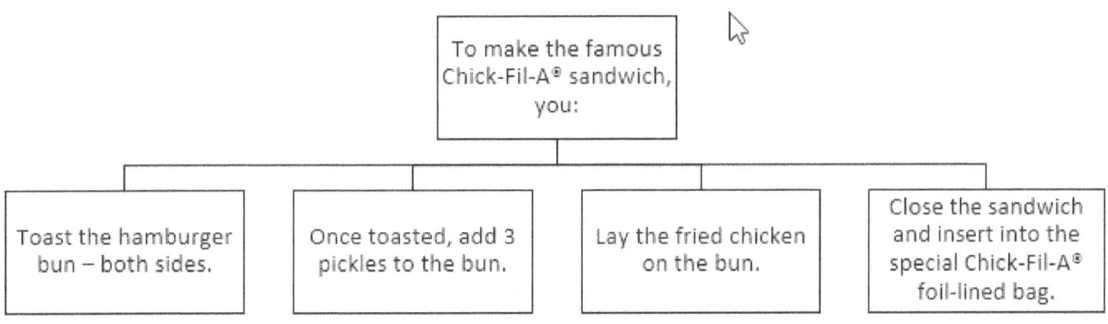

Note: this is NOT the 'official' way to make a this sandwich - it's simply an example – my perception of the process given how many of them I have enjoyed over the years – to get your juices flowing.

The process outlined above will certainly accomplish the goal. So, as a manager, you've done your job!

Leaders, on the other hand, focus on sharing vision, aligning people, driving change, encouraging risk-taking, fostering learning, enabling growth, and inspiring others.

As a leader, you'll find that much of your time is spent working to help associates understand the *why* behind the tasks they are assigned and how those tasks tie to the overall mission and organizational goals.

So, the leader's conversation with that same new associate may be more like this:

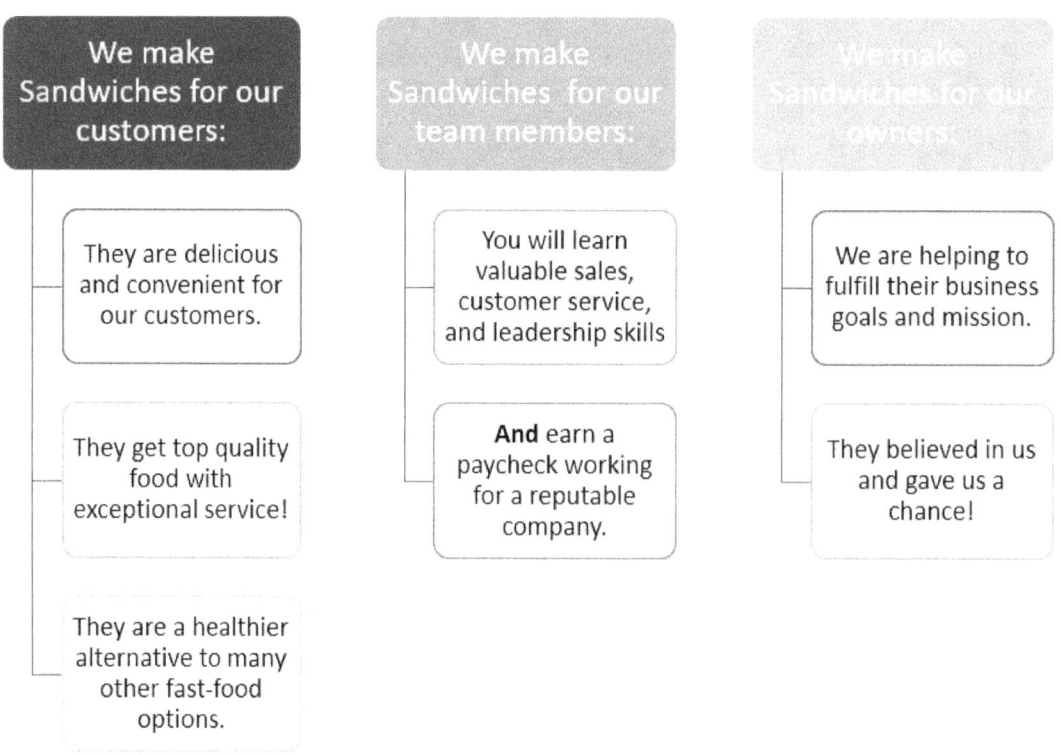

Now that new employee understands *why* making the Check-Fil-A® sandwich is an important task and what's in it for him. Leader, job well done!

LeaderShipWrecked©

In many roles, perhaps even your role, we have to learn to manage and lead concurrently, or at least consecutively. And that can be hard. Our brains tend to want to do one or the other. We have to work at doing them together. We have to be intentional with our approach and not trot through our day on autopilot making instant decisions and spewing out answers.

Consider the acts of breathing and thinking.

Both are clearly quite distinctive and separate tasks, but we can't be someone who breathes but does not think. And we can't be someone who thinks but does not breathe.

To function as human beings, we need to be capable of both breathing and thinking. In exactly the same way, people in business must be capable of both managing and leading.

Managers who cannot or will not lead will lose the confidence of their colleagues and subordinates. Leaders who do not know how to manage will sooner or later be undone by their lack of technical knowledge and competence.

It's likely you already know how to be a manager. But if not, you're going to need a different book because that's not what this book is about.

On the remainder of these pages, we're going to stay focused on being a leader, not just now but into the future!

CHAPTER 2:
A BORN LEADER?
BULLSHIT!

Remember in chapter 1 when we said leadership must be earned and developed over time?

It drives me absolutely insane when I hear people say that someone is a born leader. That's total bull shit! No one is a BORN LEADER. Leaders *aren't born*.

Was the leader you thought of earlier a leader at birth? Perhaps he or she was born with some leadership traits, but leaders aren't *born*, they are *developed*.

Think about the people you went to elementary or middle school with – in particular, the ones you thought at the time were the leaders of the pack on the playground or the ones who would most likely be successful. You know, those kids who decided what game to play at recess or set the 'what the cool kids are wearing' trends. The ones you wanted to be around, to be like.

Where are they now? Some of them may be successful now – but not all of them are leaders. Those that displayed leadership qualities early on and didn't work to grow those skills, are likely not leading anyone now.

There was this kid I went to elementary school with that everyone said would 'go places.' I remember hearing teachers, and even some of my friends' parents, talk about this kid being a 'born leader.'

Fast forward a few years and he flunked out of college and spent his adulthood working 3rd shift at a 7-Eleven. There's nothing wrong with that at all; making a living however you choose to do it is respectable. But was he a born leader? Nope.

I worked with a girl in my restaurant career who was a behind-the-scenes kind of girl. She just wanted to come to work, do her job as quietly and unobtrusively as possible, and go home. Again, respectable. That was her choice. And it was in line with her personality.

Ten+ years later, I crossed paths with her again. She was a VP responsible for overseeing a portfolio of apartment properties.

When we reconnected, I spent some time with her and learned that she had made the choice to be a leader in this new-to-her field and spent several years watching, reading, learning, and developing her leadership skills.

She wasn't 'born' to lead but she developed into a leader with hard work and practice. Because she *chose* to be a leader. Remember that from earlier?

Do you think the leader you named was seen as a leader by his/her co-workers at his/her first job? Maybe, to some degree. But most of us have to work at being great leaders.

You may be born with some leadership traits, but if you don't CHOSE to be a leader, CHOSE to use those traits, and work to grow them, you won't BE a leader.

Because **leaders aren't born**.

CHAPTER 3:
BAD LEADER BULLSHIT

I promise, every chapter in this book doesn't contain bullshit in the title but it's such a fitting word for what I'm about to talk about (just like it fit the whole 'born leader' BS in the last chapter.)

My supervisor at my first job used to say, 'There is no such thing as a bad leader.'

To me at the time, that meant that if you made the effort, you were a leader, regardless of how good you were at it.

A few years later, when I finally had the opportunity to work with a *real* leader, I understood the issue with that statement. It takes more than effort to be a leader. Just because you want to be a leader or think you are, or try to be, doesn't mean you *are* a leader.

So, the statement 'there is no such thing as a bad leader' is true but not for why you think!

It's kind of like being pregnant. You either are or you aren't. There is no 'little bit.' There is no middle ground.

It's like playing basketball. The ball either goes through the net or it doesn't. There are no points for hitting the rim.

You are either a leader or you're not. A 'bad leader' is not a leader. If you are bad at leading, you are not a leader.

Sure, there are better leaders. There are GREAT leaders. The scope of leadership can go from adequate to superb, but it can't be bad. It simply can't be.

To be a bad leader is to not be a leader at all.

Darren is the owner of a small regional hotel chain. He prides himself on staying closely involved in the day-to-day operations at all 5 of his locations. He thinks he's a leader. If there were such a thing as a bad leader, he'd be it. But he's no leader. Far from it.

He rarely seeks out feedback from his employees, and when he does, it's perfunctory; he doesn't *heed* their input. They dread his visits, he doesn't inspire them to think for themselves or seek growth opportunities, and he has made it very clear to each of them that growing the company revenue is **the** most important aspect of their job.

The customer service ratings, as you can imagine, are not good at his hotels. His employees aren't empowered to make decisions, so customers have to wait for Darren to give them an answer. The budgets are tight and crafted to preserve the asset only – not please the customer or enhance services. And he's not very understanding of the occasional sick day or family emergency that his employees deal with.

He thinks he's a leader because he's an owner. He thinks he's a leader because he has employees. Darren thinks he's a leader because he's part of the hospitality trade association's board of directors.

But he's not a leader.

He's not because there is no inspiration or service in his dealings with others. And leadership is all about inspiration and service.

Darren isn't even a likable guy, and likability is another key component of leadership.

The employee turnover at Darren's company is high.

Surprised?

The housekeeping staff are like the waves of the ocean. They come and go almost daily. The maintenance staff is sub-par because no self-respecting service technician will stay for long.

One of the longest-term managers just recently left. She told me that she took a job at a smaller hotel for a lower salary. When I asked what pushed her to do that, her response was this:

'I want to work for someone I can be proud to follow. I didn't want to follow Darren anywhere.'

Well, there you go. She didn't want to follow him so he can't be a leader. Darren is not a bad leader. He's simply not a leader at all.

Marissa is a shift leader at a large call center. She's one of 20 shift leaders the company currently employs so while she has supervisory responsibilities, it could be said that she's a small fish in a big pond.

She's been with the company only about 15 months. She does a great job, is looked to for guidance from the other shift leaders, and the customer service reps talk practically non-stop about Marissa's impact on the morale and culture of the organization.

Marissa, even though she's not in a top-level position, is a true leader. She listens to the employees, seeks out feedback and input from others, provides ongoing feedback to her team (both positive and constructive), and she takes every opportunity available to let others have the spotlight.

I had the pleasure of attending the holiday luncheon at Marissa's company and even though I knew she was a leader prior to that, her actions during that event solidified that.

Marissa was one of the last in line to eat. After devouring a small plate of food, she started circling the room, refilling tea glasses, taking away plates, and chatting with the team members. *She* was serving *them*.

Marissa's shift had one of the lowest turnover rates in the company, and the call-out percentage was less than 5%, meaning that Marissa's team rarely took an unscheduled PTO day.

There are a ton of other KPIs that Marissa's company uses to measure performance and productivity, and Marissa's team is in the top 5 of all of them and has the top spot in quite a few.

Not only is Marissa rightfully one of the company's superstars, but she is also a true leader.

CHAPTER 4:
LEADERSHIP WRECKED

Why Is It Wrecked?

It's wrecked because nothing stays the same; everything changes. And when we don't adapt to the changes around us, our followers will abandon ship (A.K.A. find someone else to follow).

Seriously, think about it. After all the crap we went through during the pandemic, and with the economic challenges since then, the workforce has changed in just about every aspect. Employee values and perspectives have changed. Most of us are more purpose driven than we have ever been. We're less tolerant than we were in the past. And our emotions are just barely under the surface these days.

Organizations have changed. Policies have changed. Processes are streamlined. Some unnecessary or redundant tasks have been eliminated. Some positions have been eliminated. AI has replaced some real people. KPIs have changed in some cases. "Work" doesn't look the same as it did a few years ago.

Decision makers don't face the same issues they did 10 years ago. Company cultures change, the mission changes, the vision changes. Everything changes. Everything.

Change is inevitable. We know that.

And as we stated earlier, part of a leader's role is to drive change. But we cannot drive change the same way we've always done it.

The truth is leadership isn't wrecked for everyone. But if you've thought of yourself as a leader for more than a few years and you haven't transformed your leadership approach, **yours is wrecked**. And it's likely that it's wrecked so badly that it won't carry you into the next year, must less beyond that.

Let me explain what I mean by wrecked.

Leadership is a never-ending journey. We don't arrive. We don't 'get there.' We have to keep practicing, working at it, honing our leadership skills. We have to develop our leadership ability. You know that or you wouldn't be reading this book. Again, I applaud you!

Whether you consciously chose to be a leader or just woke up one day and realized you were already on the boat and elected to stay there, you probably charted a course for your leadership back then. Most of us do. Even if it is just in our head, we think about what we want to use our leadership skills to accomplish and how we plan on doing it.

Very few of us, once that course is charted, make changes to it. It just becomes part of who we are and what we do, and we stop actively thinking about the process.

But think about this.

Let's say that we're steering a boat. We leave one shore with a plan to arrive safely at another shore in a different place. But along the way, the tide changes, the current becomes stronger, the wind churns up, and it becomes harder and harder to stay the course.

What do you do? Just stick with your original course, no matter how hard it gets? And regardless of how much time it adds to your trip? Or the risks you'll face that you didn't prepare for?

Or do you chart a new course?

What if the course you originally charted has you stuck in one spot, unable to get past the current pull, and unable to backtrack out of it? You're just stuck, essentially floating along making no headway at all.

Perhaps your ship runs aground.

Well, here's where I tell you that I know very little about boats, or sailing, or any of that nautical stuff. But what I do know is that it makes no sense to stay in the same place if there is an option to chart a new course.

I don't know who said it originally but:

> If we were meant to stay in one place,
> we'd have roots instead of feet.

If you wanted your boat to stay in that same spot, you wouldn't continue to fight the current. You'd drop anchor!

If you don't want your ship to go adrift, you have to take control and find a different approach.

If you never really wanted to arrive at the other shore, you'd have never left the first one.

As we've already determined, leadership ability has to be developed. And practiced. And refined. It's a never-ending expedition.

The catalyst for a fresh wave of development – the charting of a new course – is your boat being stuck on its existing course. Frustratingly, we don't always realize our leadership is wrecked until we run aground or end up some where we didn't mean to go.

Here's a real-life example.

I was working with a client that was having a terrible time getting her team to engage with her.

Carol had been brought in from the outside to take on a management position that several internal candidates had applied for. There is almost always some level of animosity in those situations. You know, the 'Why her? Why not me?' issue.

Carol was a seasoned professional with decades of experience with her previous company but six months into her new role, she was still saying frequently, 'at XXX, we did it this way,' and people were quite simply tired of hearing that.

Even though she had a lot of experience, much of Carol's experience was with one firm, and that didn't help her credibility much. There was a good bit of scepticism in her team which created more push-back than Carol had ever really dealt with.

The underlying issue though was much more fundamental.

In the very first conversation I had with Carol, I asked her to describe how she had approached the team when she first joined them. What were those first few days and weeks like? What conversations took place?

Carol's response was lengthy, but the first sentence of that response spoke volumes. She said, 'I approached the team the same way I always have, with respect and compassion.'

I hope the big gulp that statement elicited from me wasn't audible but I'm sure she saw some evidence of it on my face.

When she was wrapping up the account of her first few weeks with the team, she stated another biggie. She said, 'I guess it wasn't a good approach to assume that I could interact with them the same way I had interacted with my old team.'

Yep. Nailed it.

Carol's previous team had been with her for a while and knew her well. And they were all quite seasoned like Carol.

This new team didn't know Carol and were less experienced in their roles. The new team was very contemporary in their approach to their work, and Carol's traditional leadership approach wasn't working with them.

I could give you a dozen more examples just like this one. Mature* leaders tend to stay with their charted course but as things change, that isn't going to work.

*Mature here doesn't indicate age or generation. It refers to the type of experience and professional maturity a person has, not how many years they've been in a role or how old they are.

Contemporary Application
of Traditional Competencies

In order to right the ship – to salvage our wrecked leadership - we must understand that while there are many components of leadership that will stand the test of time, they may look different today (and tomorrow) than they did a few years ago.

A decade ago, when people talked about leadership competencies, they talked about things like fairness, modesty, and openness. And we said earlier that words like example, inspiration, vision, and influence were important components of leadership.

We also said that leaders focus on aligning people, driving change, encouraging risk-taking, fostering learning, and enabling growth.

Those competencies still apply. But they have to be *applied* differently. Contemporary associates in today's workforce don't think of those things the same way as the workforce did in the past.

Read that sentence again:

Contemporary associates in today's workforce don't think of those things the same way as the workforce did in the past.

In the next few chapters, we'll explore the contemporary application of some of the fundamentals of leadership, but I have a favor to ask of you first.

Open your mind.

Really OPEN it. WIDE OPEN.

Try to let your preconceived leadership approach and ideas fall to the side. At least for now.

Be OPEN to a different way of thinking; be ready to discover a new perspective. Not every idea or concept you read in the coming pages will fit your world or your style; that's OK. But if we aren't willing to consider an alternative approach, our ship will be tossed around in that current until it wrecks, and a wrecked ship often falls apart and becomes unsalvageable.

We don't want to be shipwrecked! And we certainly don't want to be unsalvageable!

OK, well maybe some days, being shipwrecked on a deserted island doesn't sound all that bad. But if you chose to lead, you know you can't lead when you're all alone – *it takes followers to lead.*

CHAPTER 5:
FAIR IS FAIR.
OR IS IT?

Fair in the ship world means a smooth curve such as the line of hull of the ship. And there is some correlation to leadership there. When things seem fair to everyone, the workforce sails along smoothly with the water flowing smoothly over the hull.

But that typically doesn't last long.

At some point, the water will become choppy, and the sailors will become restless and anxious.

In the late nineties and early two-thousands, when we talked about fairness in leadership, the premise was that everyone was treated fairly – AKA *the same*.

Today 'fair' doesn't mean the 'same.' Fair doesn't have the same meaning for every person. How we define fairness has a lot to do with how we were raised, what our values are, what we've experienced, and how we process others' actions.

What is equal is not always fair. What is fair is not always equal. Equal means exactly alike. Fair means in accordance with the rules or standards.

Today's leader needs a basis for how to apply 'fairness' to the followers they deal with. The more diverse the followers, the broader the perception of fairness will be.

And it's not just about fairness. Leaders must be fair-*minded.* That means we have to strive for fairness in our interactions with others, but that fairness has to be intentional and as individualized as possible, not standardized.

Being fair-minded means adopting and refining clear and sensible thinking to consider both sides of an issue *before* deciding or landing on an opinion. Fair-minded leaders make evidence-based decisions, not emotion-based decisions. And the fair-minded leader stays impartial, keeping their personal prejudices out of the mix.

The biggest chunk of my career prior to being a business owner was in the apartment industry. In the multi-family world, there are the people who develop the apartment communities – the Developers. And the people who manage the apartment communities after they are built – the Property Management Operations people.

In many organizations where there is a department for development and a department for operations, the developers are the golden geese and operations folks are the red-headed stepchildren. There is a divide between the developers and the operations team. And there is a common perception. That perception is that the developers are treated as if they are smarter and more important than the operations people. And the operations folks often feel like they work harder than the developers because they don't 'leave' the property when it's finished – the operations folks were in it for the long haul.

At the end of most projects, the development team and the operations team would sit down and talk about what worked well and what didn't, and what could be done differently next time. These meetings usually covered the gamut from the relationship between development and ops, to the communication challenges (usually the lack thereof), to other tactical issues, and to floorplan layouts and common area matters.

As an example: Operations would try to help the developers see why a particular floorplan was harder to lease than others, while the developers would question the sales and marketing ability of the ops team.

The ops team would point the finger at the developers for building a layout that was undesirable. The development team would point the finger at the ops team for not having the sales skills to lease a desirable floorplan.

Once you had been in one of these meetings, you typically went into future ones with your defenses up. Often being in one of these meetings made you feel like you were on a ship during a death roll. And if the captain didn't stop the roll soon enough the whole boat would capsize, and nothing would be accomplished outside of self-preservation.

You see, there was very little fair-mindedness in the interactions between operations and development. The developers were mostly unwilling to accept that something about what they had created wasn't perfect. And operations didn't understand much about what went into developing an apartment property, but they felt that if they couldn't lease it, it was a flaw in the product. There was widespread unwillingness to see both sides of the coin. Neither side was willing to see past their own personal prejudices about the other to actually *work* together.

To lead effectively today, we must work to see **both sides** before we make assumptions, staying impartial and keeping our own feelings and partialities out of the decision-making process.

CHAPTER 6:
MODESTY VS. HUMILITY

Previously, I mentioned modesty as a competency that has historically been associated with leadership.

But when we talked in the past about modesty as a critical leadership competency, it was often used interchangeably with humility.

Both are important leadership competencies. However, they are not the same thing.

On the surface, modesty and humility seem so similar that the words could be used interchangeably. And I know that the dictionary says that humility and modesty are synonyms, but they send a different message, certainly to today's workforce.

Modesty

Modesty refers to a person's view of themselves. A person is modest when they do not openly boast or brag and when they tend to downplay their own abilities. It's a way of not being showy with one's skills or knowledge, not gloating or putting on airs. Modesty is typically a desire to not put oneself in the spotlight so as not to be the center of attention.

And let's face it, modesty is an old-fashioned term. It describes your mom not wanting anyone besides your daddy to see her undergarments. That concept - modesty in that respect - is no longer a thing in our society, is it?

I mean, a quick look at fashion trends and you know it's true. Uber-short skirts. Bra straps are shown on purpose. Black bras worn under light colored or sheer blouses. Products being sold with sex appeal. Public talk about issues that used to be saved for behind-closed-door conversations. There really is no modesty left.

There are leaders who are white-knuckling modesty. It's been part of their leadership DNA for so long, they can't seem to let it go. Modesty can lead a leader to stay behind the scenes and/or out of the trenches, thinking that gives their associates the opportunity to be in the spotlight. And that works sometimes.

But in the contemporary workplace, that 'behind the scenes' concept can create the perception that leaders are 'above it' or 'too good' to be in the trenches. And that perception can sink your ship pretty quickly.

Humility

On the other hand, humility is more about how someone feels about his or her position as it relates to others. It's having the capacity to accept others' authority, intelligence, knowledge, or superiority without trying to challenge it or one-up them. **A person is humble when they defer to others and show a willingness to submit to others ideas, opinions, or direction.**

Humility is critical to leadership because it keeps our focus on *other's needs* – which is the heart of leadership.

Today's leader needs to be WITH their team. Not behind them. Not in front of them. And certainly not out of sight. WITH them.

You see, humility is the concept that you haven't forgotten where you came from, how hard you had to work to get where you are, and the fact that you didn't do it all by yourself. THAT'S the competency the contemporary leader must possess.

Being humble helps make a leader approachable. It's what drives great leaders to spend time on the front lines, to ask for input from all around, and to actually listen to that input.

It means that your followers have seen you make mistakes, they've heard you apologize, they know you are human. And they know you are not 'above' them or above doing whatever it takes to drive the whole team to success.

The humble leader is not the 'boss' or even the 'leader.'

The humble leader operates as part of the team, whether it's smooth sailing or stormy seas.

Humility is not thinking less of yourself;
it's thinking of yourself less.
Rick Warren

CHAPTER 7: CRYSTAL CLEAR OR SLIGHTLY OPAQUE

Openness in the past was about forthright communication. It was about sharing information and being open to hearing other's opinions and ideas. That still applies, for sure!

But in today's workforce, it's not just openness leaders need, it's translucency.

Nope, that's not a typo. **Translucency**, *not* transparency.

I know. I know. Transparency is all the rage these days. Everybody is talking about it. Organizations promote their transparency like they promote their best product or most popular service. Self-professed leaders work to maintain a 'high level of transparency' or boast about their 'transparent communication.'

But here's the thing. Transparency implies that everything can be seen. It says we're operating in a way that allows others to see our actions and hear all our words. ALL of them.

Transparency implies open communication, accountability, and NO SECRETS.

Transparency?

There's <u>internal transparency</u> meaning within the confines of the organization, transparency is practiced. And there's <u>external transparency</u> meaning the effort is being made to be transparent to the public. But we rarely hear those more defined terms. We simply hear 'transparency.'

And without clarification and full understanding of the intent, today's employees are skeptical. They don't believe organizations and leaders are fully transparent. They don't buy it and the more you try to sell it to them, the more they don't believe.

Add to that the fact that the word **transparency**, along with the concept, has been overused and misused so much in recent years. And that just adds to the skepticism around the concept.

True transparency can mean less bad behavior because there is more action exposure. But it doesn't completely rule out bad behavior or malicious actions because, well, humans are flawed. Transparency is meant to illuminate facts surrounding actions and decisions. But just because we can see the facts doesn't mean we understand why they are what they are. Or why something happened the way it did.

Hard-core transparency can impact trust levels. I mean, if everything is transparent, then doesn't that include actions that were previously confidential? And if your followers don't trust that you will protect their confidentiality, will they trust you in other areas?

Leaders who are too transparent – share too much information – create unwanted, and often unneeded stress for their team members. And that can backfire big time.

And then there's this: Leaders and organizations that achieve high levels of transparency can create a culture of finger pointing; an environment where people are routinely thrown under the proverbial bus. This happens because associates know that in order to maintain transparency, the guilty party – the wrong-doer – must be exposed. So, to prevent that transparent spotlight from pointing in their direction (just in case they've not crossed a T or dotted an I), they rat out their co-worker.

Unfortunately, that ratting out is sometimes misplaced, causing the innocent to suffer through the investigation process and subsequent reputation damage. And it doesn't take a rocket scientist to know that is just wrong. It's wrong for the individual being thrown under the bus and for the overall team. That kind of internal turmoil can do way more damage than not being transparent ever did!

I worked with an organization a few years ago that boasted extremely high transparency. It's pretty much all they talked about. And from what I could see, it was pretty close to true internal transparency. They shared everything with everyone on the inside.

At the time I was working with them, the owner of the company was trying to decide if eliminating one of the departments and outsourcing the tasks of that department would be better for the overall financial health of the organization. Because they were so transparent, everyone in the company knew this was a topic of discussion.

Sounds honest and open and good on the surface, right?

I was hired to help them figure it out. You know, to get a neutral perspective with an in-depth feasibility study.

When I started working with the team, there was already widespread fear among all the front-line employees, not just the ones in the department that might be eliminated. That fear was being driven by the transparency; by the fact that everyone knew that a department might be eliminated. Less tenured workers in other departments started worrying that they would be laid off so the company could retain more seasoned workers from the department that might go away.

Once I started digging in and the associates became comfortable talking to me, I realized how rampant and deep the fear was. It was palpable. And it became clear that the shift supervisors and team leads were making decisions as if their department wouldn't be there for long.

We kept trying to reassure the employees that no one would be put out on the streets with no warning and that we were months away from deciding. And that even if the decision was to eliminate the department, it would take months to work through the outsourcing. We did everything we could to ease their fear. Everything except promise they would keep their job. That we couldn't do.

Within a week of the discussions starting, several top performers had given notice. By the end of the first month of the feasibility study, almost 7% of their entire workforce had quit or given notice.

That may not sound like a lot but in an organization of 375, over 25 people were gone. Most of those were in the department we were evaluating which practically crippled that department.

In the end, the total transparency made the decision for them. They couldn't keep the department alive with so many open positions. And it didn't make sense to hire replacements if the department may go away in the near future. So, they shut it down, laying off 30 more associates.

That not only confirmed the fear so many associates had expressed, it caused the company to go back on their word of giving the associates plenty of notice if positions were eliminated.

I went ahead and finished the analysis because, well, they had already paid for it, and quite frankly, I was very curious as to the outcome. As it turns out, it was more lucrative for the company to keep the tasks that department was doing in-house and just streamline some of the operational components.

But it was too late.

The transparency they were so proud of did that department in.

TRANSLUCENCY.

If something is opaque, you can't see through it at all. If it's transparent, you can see through it clearly. Where the smart leader – the contemporary, realistic leader – needs to land is somewhere in between.

Hence, translucency.

If something is translucent, you can see some things but not all things. And as hip and trendy as the whole transparency fad has been, it's not only unrealistic, it's often not in the organization's best interest.

Leaders must consider the impact of transparency and if – likely **when** – the impact is riskier than helpful; they must seek to find an appropriate place in translucence.

Translucence allows leaders to be strategic with their communication. That doesn't mean it is permission for secrecy. Or that it's OK to cover up the embarrassing stuff. There still needs to be free-flowing information and honesty, especially as it pertains to organizational mission, vision, and initiatives. But savvy translucence prevents mass-chaos when decision makers are working to identify the action courses that widely impact the workforce. And it allows for higher employee satisfaction and engagement.

To find the proper level of translucence, leaders should ask themselves these questions:

- What information needs to be shared about a pending change and why?

- What risks could arise if it's shared?

- What risks could arise if it is not shared until later?

- What value does the information provide to the team? To productivity? To the organization at large?

- Does the organization have the capacity to field individual questions in a one-on-one environment once the information is shared?

- What if the information leads to a no-action result and we've already shared it?

- How will that impact the culture, trust, and engagement of our associates?

The answers will be different for each situation, and the organizational culture must be a factor in finding the right level. But it's certainly more realistic than full transparency.

CHAPTER 8:
LEADING BY EXAMPLE DOESN'T WORK THE WAY YOU THINK

Ask anyone over the age of 35 to give you five traits of a good leader and chances are, one of those traits will be 'leading by example.' It's one of the oldest core values of leadership.

A few years ago, when I first started struggling with the concept that leadership as we knew it was outdated – that it had shipwrecked many of us on an island called 'The way we've always done it' – I was presenting a keynote at a client's annual conference. The theme was – you guessed it – leadership. And it was the first time, and hopefully the only time, that I had to work very hard not to lose my shXX in front of a room full of several hundred of my client's employees.

What caused me to almost lose it on that stage that day?

I asked the audience to shout out the words or characteristics that came to mind when they thought of being a leader. And several folks shouted out 'lead by example.' That part was OK – I had expected it and had a follow-up question ready.

As the follow-up, I asked the crowd to tell me what they meant by leading by example. The response to THAT question was what caused my whole body to stiffen and my inner voice to start screaming at the top of its little lungs. The responses were:

- Walking the walk; talking the talk
- Act in the same way you expect them to act
- Do what they want others to do

Ugh. I have so many issues with all 3 of those phrases. But the biggest issue is that the execution of those concepts is often flawed. VERY flawed.

And those phrases are the epitome of 'The way we've always done it' in my opinion!

We tend to think that leading by example means that if we do our job well, those who see that will do their job well, too. The default expectancy is that you as the leader will act in a way that you believe should be the standard and others will follow suit.

The whole concept of 'lead by example' implies that we are doing everything exactly the way it is supposed to be done. But that implies that there is one 'best way' and that everyone should do it that way.

But that's not how it works.

We don't get to decide what lesson a follower learns from our actions (or our 'example') because everyone's brain processes what they observe differently. And we can't know when they will choose to learn from what they see.

Your actions may inspire others, they may set the standard for behavior, and hopefully your actions will support the culture, mission, vision, and values of the organization.

But the reality is **your actions don't lead others.**

You've heard this before: you can lead a horse to water, but you can't make him drink.

Well, thinking about that horse, if we just walk towards the water hoping the horse will follow, he may never get there. Because the example of how to walk to the water isn't what the horse needs.

And it's not what our team needs.

That horse needs us to walk to that water source with him and splash some in his face, so he knows it's there!

If you have kids, you've probably experienced a time when your child expressed displeasure that they had to go to bed while you were still up doing stuff. Consider the 'example' that sets for the child.

It's not realistic though that you go to bed at the same time as the child (even though we may want too sometimes!) It's not about setting the *example* of what to do, it's about setting *the standard of behavior*.

Our followers don't need us to lead with the example we want them to see. They need us to lead by supporting the mission and values of the company and by holding them accountable for that mission and those values.

Sure, we have to consider what others see us do and say. So yes, we have stayed aligned with the standards. You can call that *an* example if you want to.

But if you must hold onto the concept of setting *the* example, it has to be about the example that your team needs to see, not the one you want them to see. Remember, it's about them, not you.

In the spotlight

A colleague was talking about technology the other day and made the observation that he felt like 'leading by example' was far more important today than it has ever been. He was referring to the concept that everything ends up in a video or social media post these days.

It's true - in today's technology-focused world, someone is always watching you and what they see matters. Every leader is in the spotlight all the time everywhere they go. Someone is always watching, both internally and externally.

Others in your organization, even those who don't report to you, work with you, or even interact with you, are watching to see what you do. There are tons of people watching that you don't know are watching.

They are watching for screw ups, to see if you freak out under pressure and to see how you treat others. They are looking when you make a risky decision, while you ponder your options, and when you think nothing you are doing is watch-worthy.

And watching is easier now than it's ever been because much of what we do ends up on social media for the world to see. That is true especially when what we've done is really great or really wrong. The mediocre stuff doesn't make for a juicy newsfeed, but you can bet the mistakes and flubs are great Facebook fodder.

So sure, we can never forget that someone is watching us, and we need to make sure that what they see will make us proud of ourselves. But our energy really needs to be on setting the standard of work quality, not just through our own actions, but through communication, procedures, and accountability.

I can't think of a single time ever when I saw a leader do something (either in person or on social media) when I said, 'I want to do *exactly* what that person did.' THAT would be an example.

I *can* think of hundreds of times when I saw a leader's actions and was inspired to make a change in my own behavior. THAT'S setting the standard!

CHAPTER 9: INSPIRATION, VISION, AND INFLUENCE

Inspiration

That word means something different to different people. A great leader knows his direct followers well enough to at least have an idea of what inspires them. But depending on how big the follower pool is, it might not be possible for you to know all of your followers. And that means that we have to inspire in numerous ways in order to reach as many people as possible.

At the core of inspiration is enthusiasm.

Enthusiasm – excitement, intensity, eagerness, enjoyment - is inspiring in so many ways to so many people. Without it, you will find it hard to be a great leader.

I don't mean that cheerleader-type rah-rah-rahs are required. That's not the kind of enthusiasm I'm talking about. I'm talking about finding joy in your work, doing it with a hearty spirit, and staying positive through challenging times. Having *authentic gusto* for the mission will be evident in the way we approach our work. That's the kind of enthusiasm that speaks to just about everyone and can be inspiring for the long haul.

The energy your followers apply to their jobs is directly tied to your enthusiasm for the mission and if we don't have a fairly high level of passion for the mission, we need to find another mission.

Vision

Contemporary leaders have to have vision. I'm not talking about their eyeballs being able to see; I'm talking about being able to envision what tomorrow and next month and next year will look like. And how we'll get there together.

Fostering a sense of connection and belonging so that the team can succeed as a collective has to be at the core of the vision.

Your followers want to know that you have a plan. And they want you to share it with them. Many of today's workforce will corner you on that and if you can't pony up the future vision details, they'll move on to a leader who can.

So, we have to hone our visionary skills. If you only have the capacity to put out today's fires and aren't spending at least some of your energy planning for next year, and the year after that, you may find it difficult to keep your followers engaged.

Here are some tips for developing a visionary approach (borrowed from some of the fabulous visionaries I am privileged to know.)

1. Try looking at everything from an outsider's point of view – sort of a forget-what-you-know approach so that your own perceptions and experiences aren't getting in the way of finding a better solution or fresh approach.

2. It takes innovation to be a visionary. Apply a current process to a completely different task. Or take a task back to a manual process and work your way to a more

efficient solution. Knowledge alone won't set the world on fire. Finding a new, better way to do something will!

3. Gather data and use it but don't forget to look past the data, too. Gather feedback from everyone you can, and then gather some more. The best ideas don't come from spreadsheets, they come from people!

4. Don't be a 'why' person. Be a 'why not' person. If someone says 'that won't work' ask why not. If you feel like you can't accomplish something, why not? If a solution that seemed to be a great option isn't working, ask why not? If we just accept something without a challenge, won't we just keep doing things the same way we've always done them?

Influence

Someone once told me that influence is about getting someone else to do something that they don't want to do without asking or telling them to do it. Essentially getting them to volunteer to do it.

But that's a bit slinky for my taste. I prefer Webster's definition. Webster's Dictionary says influence is *the capacity to have a positive impact on the character, development, or behavior of someone, and that's what our followers are looking to us to do – have an impact on them in some constructive way.*

That influence factor is why leadership isn't about your role or your responsibility level. It's about others.

> The key to successful leadership today is
> influence, not authority.
> Kenneth Blanchard

I once worked for an organization that really didn't have their act together. They didn't have ducks in a row, they had a bunch of laughing hyenas who were having a party every day at work. What I saw during the interview process was nothing like what I saw on day one.

At the end of the first day I drove home burdened with thoughts of regret and anxiety over what I was going to do. I needed a job so I just couldn't just up and quit but this new place sure didn't seem like the place for me.

But as I said, I had to have a paycheck, so I went back the second day – against the advice of that little voice in my head. And on that second day, I met someone who would have a powerful widespread ongoing positive impact on me for many years to come.

Katie was a fish out of water at that place, too, but she had contagious energy and passion for everything she did. She was one of those people that you could tell was just happy to be alive every single day and could take on whatever came her way because of it.

Katie was inspiring and uplifting and saw the best in everyone, even if they couldn't see it in themselves.

And she listened. I mean, she *really listened* to everything anyone said to her. She was never too busy to do something for someone else, yet she always managed to get her job done (and did it well, I might add.)

She wasn't my direct supervisor; in fact, Katie wasn't anyone's boss. She was a one-women department, but she was the go-to person for a lot of us. And she quickly became my mentor.

It was her influence that led me to stick with my job there for a little bit to learn some things I might not ever get the chance to learn again.

She didn't tell me I should stay. Through our conversations I realized that while it felt like chaos, there were some really innovative things going on in that company that could benefit me later in my career and she was right!

THAT'S INFLUENCE, PEOPLE!

She also was the one who helped me realize that consensus is overrated and really doesn't belong in a leader's toolbox.

I was meeting with my team one day and had asked Katie to sit in since her department would be impacted by a change we needed to implement. After talking with the team about what needed to change, I felt good about the meeting. There had been very few questions, almost no pushback, and everyone seemed to be onboard.

I told Katie as we were walking back to our offices that I was pleased with how things went. I asked her what she thought. She mentioned seeing a lot of nodding heads as I was talking, and I agreed with a level of self-satisfaction that, I'd learn later, was misplaced.

In my mind, if people were nodding their heads, they were at least listening, and I chose to believe that it also meant they agreed. I said as much to Katie.

Who then replied by asking me if I needed people to agree with me or if I needed people to poke holes and brainstorm on alternative options? I pondered that for a minute and then it hit me.

What I wanted was for people to agree with me. What I NEEDED was for the people on my team to think for themselves, share their ideas, and pick apart the plan with what-ifs. I didn't need a bunch of yes-men on my team; I needed thinkers, doers, hole-pokers, and questioners.

If everyone in the room is nodding in agreement, they aren't thinking of alternative options or better solutions and that's not what we need.

Katie had helped me see that by asking one simple question. I had gotten caught up in my authority and wanting to be the one with the answers. I had unintentionally created a team environment where no one felt comfortable challenging my ideas. And let me tell you, it took a lot of work to undo that but thanks to Katie's influence, I was at least aware of the issue and was able to start the work of fixing my mess!

CHAPTER 10:
NAVIGATING CHANGE

Average leaders think their work is done when a decision is made.

Great leaders know that the hard part is the execution of the change. Navigating through change is one of a leader's biggest – and most challenging – opportunities.

The reality is that without change, individuals can't grow, organizations can't continue to compete, customers won't stay......

Great leaders must put energy into initiating, supporting, and implementing change. And major change calls for strategic disruption. Change creates chaos but it's the nature and severity of that chaos that great leaders learn to manage.

Being tactical about how and when information about the change is shared (the translucency we discussed earlier), having a comprehensive support system in place for the change, ensuring the WHY is discussed in detail, and allowing some of that chaos to play out are all part of strategic disruption.

We'll get back to the pieces of strategic disruption in a little bit but first, we need to talk about how to get ourselves ready for the disruption that change brings with it.

In order for leaders to become adept at navigating through change, we have to have a high level of INTENTIONALITY and ADAPTABILITY.

Intentionality

Intentionality is the act of being deliberate or purposeful. It's to move, act, decide, or interact with intention. What that intention is can vary depending on the situation but it's doing things on purpose, versus just letting things happen willy–nilly.

Being intentional doesn't mean forceful or overly firm. It's being deliberate and choosing to consider the outcome before we act. It's the same concept my Dad tried to teach me when I was little and he'd say, 'put your mind in gear before you put your mouth in motion.'

I know, it sounds like a lot of work! And it can be at first. But once we build the habit of being intentional, we'll find change is easier to manage and less scary for everyone.

Intentionality doesn't mean that we can't be afraid of change. A healthy level of fear drives us and keeps us focused. And it doesn't mean that we won't experience uncomfortableness when we stretch ourselves. But being intentional helps us make fewer mistakes because we are staying focused on the intended outcome by taking purposeful action.

The first step to being intentional is to understand your purpose. Why are on this earth? Why are you in the position you are in? Why are you where you are? What is your primary goal in being there?

Finding your purpose isn't a 5-minute process and it's one of the most important things you will ever do. You may have already figured it out. I wrote a book about how to do it if you need help. But we won't be digging into *this* book. Just know that it's a critical piece of the life puzzle AND the leadership puzzle.

Once we know our purpose, and begin aligning our thoughts, decisions, and approach with that purpose, a level of intentionality will develop without much work.

But to increase our intentionality even more, add these actions to your work:

1. Practice pausing before you make a decision, react to a question, or respond to a complaint. Give yourself time to prepare your mind, let go of prejudices, and wipe away knee-jerk reactions that aren't in keeping with intentionality.
2. Ask questions and gather feedback before developing a strategy, making a decision, or taking action.
3. Take ownership of what you do and hold yourself accountable.
4. Reflect on your actions frequently and adjust future behavior accordingly.

You won't become an intentional leader overnight, but you'll be glad when you get there!

Adaptability

The contemporary leader must possess a high level of adaptability in addition to intentionality.

Traditional leaders often focus on being the steady eddy, offering a level of consistency and stability to those they lead. Keeping an even keel has long been a source of pride for many leaders, and that can be pride-worthy.

While consistency and stability have a place in a leader's toolbox for some situations, the modern leader must be able to flex with the gracefulness of a champion gymnast.

We all know that there will be change. There is always change. It's constant and unavoidable. It's often good, but it can be bad, too. And for the contemporary leader, change of any kind takes a high level of adaptability.

To be clear, though, adapting is more than *handling* change. It's more than dealing with it or getting through it. It's more than surviving. It's *accepting* the change, *embracing* the change, and being the champion of change *even when you don't want to.*

And before you choose to skip the whole adaptability thing, consider this: Leaders who can't or won't adapt *squash flexibility in others.* That means that implementing change will be even harder for you and your team. If your followers can't see you flex, they may think it's unimportant for them to flex. And if they don't think it's important, it simply won't happen.

We can foster adaptability in ourselves and others by being inquisitive. Ask questions. Research. Ask more questions. Seek feedback and multiple alternatives.

The adaptable leader needs to plan for the change by:

Fully understanding the why behind the change so you can communicate that why to your followers.

Predicting the unknown and developing a plan for whatever that might be. Don't get too attached to Plan A. It might work out and it might not. Have a backup plan and a back-up plan for the back-up plan.

Planning for an alteration to your own behavior or approach to accommodate the change. Pay attention to your response to the changes around you. Being an adaptable leader, especially during big change, means we have to be prepared for our emotions to bubble to the surface sometimes. And being prepared for them will help you be able to manage them while remaining flexible.

Map out the communication strategy – how much information is to be shared and when; how will associates get answers to the questions you didn't answer in the official communication, and what does the support system look like

Strategic Disruption

We've talked about how great leaders put effort into driving change. And we said earlier that major change calls for strategic disruption.

Remember this paragraph?

Change creates chaos but it's the nature and severity of that chaos that great leaders learn to manage. Being tactical about how and when information about the change is shared, having a comprehensive support system in place for the change, ensuring the WHY is discussed in detail, and allowing some of that chaos to play out are all part of strategic disruption.

I'll admit it. When I first heard someone talking about strategic disruption, I thought he had lost his mind. Being such a literal thinker, strategic disruption sounds like an oxymoron to me. How can you methodically approach a disruption?

To me, a disruption was something that you didn't plan for. The person that pops in uninvited just when you're on a roll with your hardest task of the day, or the rain shower that pops up just as you get the food laid out on the picnic table. It's the coffee pot being empty when you walk into the break room, or the vending machine being out of your favorite snack. It's the line at the grocery store being super long when you are in a hurry to get home, or the traffic jam created by the big wreck on the interstate. Those were disruptions in my head. Things that happen that are beyond your control and completely unpredictable.

But if we do plan for change, we can plan for chaos – hence strategic disruption!

If we aren't willing to deal with some disruption to the normal flow of things, we won't be able to take on change because that's essentially what change does – it disrupts the way things are now.

Often, when we're going through a major organizational change, our focus is on the intended outcome, and getting everyone to adopt the change within a specific time frame. But there is so much more to it than that.

Sure, training and communication are important but the most important factor in change is the people affected by the change.

We have to be prepared for an impact to productivity, not just from an organizational outcome perspective but from an employee impact perspective. When productivity wanes, employee motivation withers and even your superstars and supporters can get frustrated.

We need to consider what will happen when employees find alternative options for the new process. And they will. If we allow the workarounds to go unaddressed, the change may fail. When other employees see there are no consequences to ignoring the new process, they may start questioning why they should be on board if others aren't. And that will significantly impact the credibility of the change driver.

Managing a big change in an organization takes a lot of planning and preparation. It takes having a detailed implementation process, and clear identification of the support structure. And it takes you as the leader, being calm and collected in the throes of the chaos that big change creates.

Here are a few action items that will help you lay the groundwork for strategic disruption.

Conduct an initial impact analysis. Define the capacity for change in the people most affected by it. Hold focus group meetings. Form a champion panel. Or create an implementation team with a mix of front-line and management associates to dig into the what-ifs and possible disruptions.

Define and communicate the WHY early on. I've implemented tons of policy and procedure changes in my career, and I can tell you without a doubt, the earlier we start talking about the WHY behind the change, the more successful the change process is. Seriously, I can't talk enough about the importance of WHY. If your followers don't understand *why* they are being asked to change, they may never really get behind it.

And the why can't be 'because it's what's best for the organization.' There has to be more to it than that.

Here's how you know if you've adequately developed the WHY communication: write down the why in one sentence. And then in response to that sentence, ask why again. Write that answer down. And then respond to that answer with why. And keep doing that until there is no more WHY left.

Once you get to that final 'why' answer, now put yourself in the employee's shoes and ask, 'what's in it for me?'

When communicating about the WHY, include the what's-in-it-for-me piece, too. That's the most important piece to your followers!

Create an implementation plan with details, timelines, task owners, and support contacts. Many times, organizations have more than one change going on at once and if one of those changes is planned poorly, it will affect all of them.

Put together an implementation team. Align people around the change based on passions, experience, personality, willingness to adapt, and capacity to lead. You don't have to do it all yourself. And you can't rely on a manager to do it all by himself either. It should be a team effort so that the associates see widespread adoption early on.

Periodically during the change, seek out feedback. How is it going? What isn't working? What could be done better? How is it helping?

You'll likely find that many people will answer with 'it's fine' or 'it's going OK' – don't settle for that. Ask for details. When I get those generic answers from my team members, I'd say, 'OK. But I'm going to ask you again in a day or two and when I do, I want details of the good and the bad.' And it worked!

Identify the Safe Place. There will be pain during the change, no matter how well you plan. Identify what your team members should do if the pain becomes unbearable or prevents them from being a productive part of the process. Who do they go to? What are their options for relief, even temporary relief? Is there a judgement-free zone where they can deal with their pain with no repercussions?

That doesn't mean the pain will go away or that the change will stop if someone needs a life preserver. It simply means that you are aware there will be some discomfort and are willing to plan for that, too.

CELEBRATE. Celebrate meeting benchmarks or deadlines throughout the change process. Even if they seem like baby steps. If you want the resisters to stay on board, you must recognize their effort by celebrating the little victories along the way.

We need to celebrate the completion too. Often, we move on to the next change as soon as one change has been 80% adopted, and that might be necessary. But our followers need to know when one is 'finished', and we need to celebrate the end of that transition.

A client I was working with shifted from manual expense report submissions to the use of automated expense reports through an app. Their implementation plan spanned 4 months, with the goal of having 25% app participation by the end of the first month, 50% by the end of the second month, etc. And at the end of each month, there was a celebratory shout out from the change leader highlighting the percentage of participation, naming, and thanking key supporters, congratulating everyone, and reminding the team of the next goal. This shout-out was in video form message and the team really responded well to that.

That organization hit their first 2 goals but at the end of the 3rd month, they were only at 72% instead of the planned 75%. And do know what the leader did? He sent the celebratory shout-out video anyway.

Sure, he mentioned that the team was a little shy, but he recognized the hard work and dedication that went into making it this far and sweetened the final goal by offering a $10.00 bonus for all employees on the first expense report after the final goal was met – as long as that goal was met by the initial deadline. But this was an all-or-nothing offer.

This guy really knew his team. I initially thought ten bucks wouldn't do much, but I was wrong. The ones who had already completed the shift to using the app were reaching out to their teammates who weren't and helping them. Not only did they make the goal, they made it 2 weeks early! And everyone got their extra ten dollars!

Now you won't always have to offer tangible incentives like that guy did. The point with sharing that story was not to make you feel like you have to 'buy' participation, but rather to enforce the impact of celebrating the small steps and to remind us all that a missed benchmark may not mean the whole process is off course!

CHAPTER 11: ALIGNING PEOPLE

Aligning people in your workforce will likely always be one of your greatest leadership challenges. When associates are not appropriately aligned with work that fits their capacity, skillset, and passion, it makes for an uphill performance battle. And that battle is one that creates burn-out and disengagement quicker than any other workplace issue.

It's one of the reasons that I am so relentless with my clients when it comes to making triple sure we have the right people in the right role. When someone is in a role that isn't right for them, job satisfaction is low, self-fulfillment takes a hard hit, and employee turnover is impacted.

The equation for appropriate people alignment is two-fold.

First, there's PURPOSE. A leader must pay attention to an individual's purpose to ensure that it aligns with the organization's purpose. If the organization's primary purpose is to provide an exceptional customer experience, then the associates must have a personal purpose and value system that aligns with that.

Great leaders will not only encourage employees to identify their personal purpose, but they will provide their followers with the means and resources to make that identification. If an employee doesn't know his or her life purpose, how can they – or you – know if they are aligned with the right role?

Not the first time you've heard that, right? Remember Chapter 10?

The second component is CLARITY. Today's leaders must set a culture of clarity in multiple ways.

Clarity in communication, expectations, and authority is critical.

Communication in all forms must be clear and variable. Clear in that today's leaders need to use plain language in written communication and the spoken word. Variable in that we have to remember not everyone processes what they hear and read the same way so we may have to convey an idea or expectation in more than one way so that we can connect with everyone's thought patterns.

Clear expectations should be set, agreed upon, and discussed often. Good leaders talk to their followers about expectations at the beginning of the relationship or when something isn't going quite right. Great leaders talk to their followers about expectations on a regular basis – from both directions – because just as you have expectations for your workforce, your associates have expectations of you, too. The only way to stay on the same page is to talk about it!

Fully understanding authority and empowerment levels is a must for productivity and employee engagement. Too many times, decisions aren't made because an employee isn't sure if she has the authority to make it, and that leads to a whole host of challenges.

Great leaders will develop a culture of clear authority that supports the company's mission and vision.

I worked for a great leader that created a culture where his workforce knew that they had the authority to resolve a customer service issue. No one was ever chastised or punished for *making a decision*. If it wasn't the right call, that would be discussed as a way to learn from the experience, but you were never 'in trouble' for deciding. Not making a decision on the other hand would put you on the hot seat!

Another leader I worked for set specific ranges for authority. For example, location managers knew that they could make customer service decisions for up to a thousand dollars without any fear of repercussions. Anything over that amount had to be discussed with an area VP first. Everyone knew what decisions they could and couldn't make because leadership had ensured clarity in that regard.

Clarity in responsibility, accountability, and how each role fit into the big picture is necessary in today's world. Today's workforce practically demands precise direction as it relates to what one is held responsible for. If an employee doesn't know he's responsible for doing something and is then questioned as to why they didn't do it, that's going to create an issue.

That's not to say we should accept behavior that demonstrates the its-not-my-job mentality. But associates have to understand what they will be held accountable for.

Charlie had been working at a retail location for a while and had recently been promoted to the assistant manager. He thought he had a good handle on his new responsibilities as did his manager.

One day, one of the sales associates just walked out mid-shift and said she wasn't coming back.

Charlie called another associate who was off that day and asked if she could come in to finish the open shift, and she did. Charlie sent an email to the manager letting her know about the girl who quit. He also checked the schedule for the next few days to ensure that the quitter wasn't scheduled to work any shifts in the coming days.

In Charlie's mind, he had handled the immediate need, notified the decision maker, and prepared for the next few days so he thought he had fulfilled his responsibilities. It was up to the manager to plan beyond that and to decide what to do about the open position.

Unfortunately, Charlie was surprised the next day when he was chastised for not completing a position requisition form and submitting it to HR. In the manager's mind, Charlie was responsible for doing that since he was the manager on duty when the employee quit. In Charlie's mind, since the form showed a signature line requiring the manager's signature, it wasn't something the assistant manager could or should do.

Several other issues like that came up and eventually, Charlie was so disillusioned that he moved on to another retail position with a different company.

If Charlie had been given more clarity regarding his responsibilities and what he would be held accountable for, he might have stayed. Instead, he is now a regional operations director for a different retailer and is definitely a superstar in his field.

Not only was Charlie not provided clarity, his situation and his manager's reaction to it may have indicated another alignment issue.

Alignment is not just ensuring the right people are in the right role. It's about making sure that those people are on board with the organizational mission. And that takes – you guessed it – purpose and clarity.

The organization has to fully understand its overall purpose and convey that purpose in everything it does.

I'll use my company as an example. As a talent development company, I provide group training, customized workshops, curriculum, train-the-trainer services, individual and team coaching, and talent related consulting. Those are the *services* I offer. They are NOT my company's *purpose.*

The purpose for my company's existence is to help organizations and individuals be better today than they were yesterday through inspiration, transformational thinking, and positive learning experiences.

If I had employees, I would need to make sure they knew that. And that we talked about it frequently.

As it is in my one-man shop, when I am struggling with a decision, I go back to my organizational purpose and see how the decision options align with it – if a choice fits with the purpose, that's the answer to my dilemma.

So, purpose added to clarity results in alignment – in people and in the organizational mission. And who doesn't love it when everything lines up perfectly!

PURPOSE added to CLARITY results in ALIGNMENT.

CHAPTER 12:
LEARNING AND GROWTH

The contemporary leader will be as focused on creating an environment conducive to professional and personal growth as they are to growing revenue. That's because today's great leaders know that creating an environment like that will organically grow the organization's revenue in a variety of ways.

To be a great leader, one must be a perpetual learner. The great JFK knew this to be true.

> Leadership and learning are
> indispensable to each other.
> John F. Kennedy

When you stop learning, you stop growing. And when you stop growing, you stop being able to lead. It's as simple as that.

What better way to continue learning and growing than creating a culture that fosters learning for everyone? Enabling growth for all followers is one of the facets that set a great leader apart from an OK one.

I've heard managers worry that if the focus is on talent development and growth, they will lose top talent to other firms.

The truly great leader knows that's a selfish approach – and virtually anything selfish is contra-leadership. Plus, when we are honestly in the leadership boat to help others, helping them cultivate their talent, expand their skills, and grow personally and professionally is really our obligation, albeit an honorable and rewarding one.

Sir Richard Branson said it best:

Train them well enough so they can leave.
Treat them well enough so
they don't want to.

Many of us get a little itchy though when we talk about creating a culture of growth and perpetual learning. The little voice in our head starts panicking and muttering about the cost, the time, the headache.... As somewhere off in the distance, we hear the angels cry as the money flows out the door for Learning Management Systems (LMS), trainers' salaries, and time away from productivity. It's like that wrecked ship we are in is taking on water (AKA the cost of training) and we're going to sink if we keep going.

But here's the reality:

Creating a culture doesn't cost anything other than effort and time. Sure, you can throw money at incentives and initiatives so you can pretend to buy the culture you're looking for. But that's not a lasting solution.

An organic culture is a longer lasting culture and takes less effort to preserve. When leaders' actions demonstrate the core values and mission, the culture grows from there.

I have a client that owns a fairly young, medium sized marketing company that oozes perpetual learning. It didn't take me long to see that their culture was organization wide, not just pocketed in a few departments.

When I asked the owner how she created a culture where everyone was so collaborative and willing and ready to learn, she answered me this way: (paraphrased slightly)

'It's really not hard; it just takes effort and dedication. I know that as a new-ish company, we will be faced with tons of changes in the coming months and years. And I want to be ready for that.

So, I make sure to discuss change and learning at length during the interview process. Lots of questions about what they learn, how they learn, why they learn, how they use what they learn. Questions about how they feel about change, how they handle it, prepare for it. And if they are hired, on day one, they work with their direct manager to develop their learning map for their first quarter.

We have an employee portal where everyone shares their learning stories and the challenges they've overcome.

Every staff meeting in each department starts with each person sharing something new they learned since the last meeting, and it has to be something of substance. You can't just say that you learned you don't like peach salsa.

I don't bring employees in for a private chat when they've missed the mark or done something wrong; I bring them in for that private chat when I don't see evidence of their growth in some manner.'

She went on to share more details with me, some of which I've incorporated into the next few paragraphs. But in those few sentences, I heard these key points:

- Creating a culture of growth takes effort and dedication – just like anything that's worthwhile.

- It requires you hire the right people to help establish and nurture the culture you are trying to create.
- Those that are hired must be started off with the right message, tools, and vision. Growth and learning must come first, and it simply must be demonstrated by how new associates are handled starting on day one.
- And there must be ongoing effort and evidence of the culture.

Completely doable but harder than it sounds.

I work with several companies that develop commercial real estate, and one of the common things that happens after a project is finished is those involved in the project will meet to discuss what worked and what didn't – essentially what they could be better or at least differently next time. (Very similar to the scenario with developers and operators I talked about in Chapter 5.)

The concept behind these project completion meetings is solid!

Unfortunately, these meetings are often focused on the minutiae like light fixtures, sub-contractors, design, window choices, and the list goes on. Those things are important, sure.

But no one in those meetings asks the big question: WHAT DID YOU LEARN FROM THIS EXPERIENCE?

If that were the first question asked in those meetings, some of the answers would be about design and the minutiae but it would also reveal some talent related growth like communication challenges that were overcome and how the various teams involved can work better together.

The decision makers who are responsible for the commercial projects they develop tend to get so wrapped up in the details of the actual product they are creating, they forget that it's the collective talent that actually makes it happen and that talent must be nurtured.

Talent development doesn't have to be expensive. And it doesn't have to be fancy.

If your organization uses a Learning Management System, that's fine. And if managed correctly, the LMS is a great tool. Sadly, many times the need to have an efficient management process for the LMS creates a training process that is blanketed across the roles with no regard to individual needs and goals.

Here's an example of that:

Let's say a company provides security services. For that organization, there are several topics that employees have to 'learn' about every year for compliance purposes and to serve as CYA for the firm. So of course, you will mandate those topics in your LMS.

But let's say that the same company also has time management, verbal communication, written communication, and telephone skills in their curriculum.

If Nancy is never late with a report, never misses a deadline, always seems to have her work done in a timely manner, and rarely has to stay late to catch up, she probably doesn't need to take time management.

She's demonstrated her ability to manage her time efficiently and to make her take a class on the subject is demeaning. It tells her you haven't noticed how well she manages her time, or worse yet, you don't care. And either one is bad!

If John is extremely adept at verbal communication but his written reports and emails are sometimes unclear, then assign written communication to him as a required course but let him skip the verbal communication one – unless he chooses to take it.

If the person that employees are looking to for guidance (YOU – their leader!) doesn't recognize their strengths and apply what they recognize to the growth process and learning requirements, they will eventually stop looking to that person for guidance. Afterall, why should they look at your actions, when you are clearly not paying attention to theirs?

The same concept applies to the type of learning opportunities you provide or encourage. Not everyone learns the same way. The great leader understands this and works to develop a mixed media approach to any required training.

Today's workforce isn't one that is going to be willing to spend hours sitting in front of their computer taking poorly constructed online courses. They simply won't do it. Sure, they may check the box by clicking through and taking the quiz at the end, but they won't learn anything from it. And that's just money AND TIME down the drain.

A blend of formal classroom, informal shadowing, hands-on, videos, self-guided learning, and collaborative or tribal learning will enhance the learning culture far more than any one of those approaches alone.

The contemporary workforce also wants to see evidence of leaders learning. They want to hear about it when you screw up – what did you do and what did you learn from it? What will be different going forward?

They want to see you in a class. They want to know that you took the online course they are made to sit through. And they need to know that you are **in it with them**. If that's a foreign concept to you at this point, I'll kindly encourage you to go back to Chapter 6 and read it again.

CHAPTER 13:
SOCIAL INTELLIGENCE, PRUDENCE, AND COURAGE

Social Intelligence

Social Intelligence (SI) is one of the best predictors of effective leadership. It's how someone interprets and responds to social situations; the ability to operate effectively in, and be sensitive to, a variety of social scenarios.

By 'social' we're not just talking about parties, social events, or events outside of work. It could be at a company function, group training, or industry event. How someone conducts themselves at any one of those is a good indicator of where someone is with their social intelligence.

If you willingly expose yourself to different people, and different situations, and if you have the ability to engage others in social conversations, especially those you don't know, that likely is an indication of a high level of SI.

Those of us who are extroverts often naturally have a high level of SI but that doesn't mean that a more introverted person can't also have high social intelligence.

Many great leaders are introverts but also have a high SI because it's about putting themselves out there, actively participating in conversations – even those that don't necessarily interest you; it's about being aware of how your actions or inactions in social settings are perceived by others.

Social Intelligence is a competency that is likely going to come easily to the younger generations since they have been so socially supported and typically have a higher level of confidence than older generations. However, their exposure to technology may mean they won't seek out these social interactions without some prompting.

Those younger generations will likely be very intolerant of low SI in their leaders. It will probably be a factor in their selection of who to follow and who not to follow.

As a leader of a contemporary workforce, we must be observant. We're going to need to observe our team members in social situations, encourage them to expand their social intelligence, push them out there in some cases, give them feedback on their interactions, and recognize those actions that exhibit a high level of SI. We won't be able to create future leaders if we don't pay attention to the social intelligence of our workforce.

Prudence

Prudence sounds like an antiquated concept; probably because we don't hear that word very often anymore. It was one of the cardinal virtues that Aristotle ranted about but you and your friends probably don't use it in conversations.

Prudence about wisdom, but more than that, it's the ability to see others' perspectives and to be open to considering someone else's points of view, even if those views are drastically different from one's own.

In the next decade, as the workforce becomes even more vocal and more diverse than it is now, prudence is going to be vital. The only way we are going to be able to lead an uber-diverse followership will be to pre-empt some conflict by being prudent.

We can expand on our prudence by really listening to others, learning to ask for other opinions, and actually considering those opinions before making decisions.

If we encourage our team members to do these things as well, we can help them expand their leadership ability and identify the future leaders within our own team.

Members of the younger generations will most definitely require the leaders they follow to exhibit prudence in their interactions with their team members. If their leaders aren't willing to really listen to and consider their ideas, they will find leaders who will.

Courage

Prudence takes courage.

Social intelligence takes courage.

Being a leader takes courage.

It takes courage to take risks, to stand up to what you believe, to do the right thing, and to be open to new ways of thinking and doing things.

It takes courage to be open to other beliefs, and the courage to make mistakes as a way of learning.

And in leadership, we often need more courage than we typically have lying around so we have to gather it up, summons it from beyond, work it up from our toes....

When I need courage – like to face a difficult conversation with someone, I ask myself this question: what's the worst thing that could happen?

Sometimes the 'worse thing' is pretty dang bad. But rarely does the worst that could happen actually end up happening. So, once I've prepared myself for the worst, what actually happens isn't so bad.

When I need courage – like when I'm meeting with a new client who I already know is going to be a tough sale – I use music.

I turn on Charlie Daniel's Devil Went Down to Georgia and crank it up loud. Then I sing along – loudly and off-key - as if I were on stage at a CDB concert. By the time I get to the part that says, 'I done told you once, you son of a bXXXX, I'm the best that's ever been,' I'm practically invincible!

Music may not work for you, but you have to find what does. FIND IT. USE IT. Build your courage however you can because you're going to need it.

It's not just us though that needs to be courageous. We have to help our followers build their courage as well.

We can help them do that by establishing a safe environment, where associates are encouraged to stand up for their beliefs, allowed to voice their opinions without fear of being chastised.

We can create a culture where associates have the autonomy to make decisions, and subsequently, mistakes, without fear of backlash.

The environment we create will help our team members build the courage they need to be great leaders.

The up-and-coming generations are probably going to demand autonomy and may willingly, if not forcefully, share their opinions. And they will expect to be heard and we're going to need the courage to let that happen.

LeaderShipWrecked©

CHAPTER 14:
NEWBIE LEADERSHIP

Hiring managers must actively choose emerging leaders for positions of authority; otherwise, we end up with people in the top positions that haven't chosen to lead and that can be catastrophic – it could land your ship in Davey Jones' locker!

DAVY JONES'S LOCKER IS A METAPHOR FOR THE OCEANIC ABYSS, THE FINAL RESTING PLACE OF DROWNED SAILORS AND TRAVELERS. IT IS A EUPHEMISM FOR DROWNING OR SHIPWRECKS IN WHICH THE SAILORS' AND SHIPS' REMAINS ARE CONSIGNED TO THE DEPTHS OF THE OCEAN.

How do we tell if someone would make a good leader during the interview process?

It can be hard. Many candidates are very good at interviewing. They say the right things and ask the right questions.

The secret is to develop a process for getting to the *evidence behind their leadership ability.*

Here is one way to identify leadership potential during the interview process that has worked well for me.

If a candidate makes it past the first interview – or whatever point in your process that indicates there is serious interest on both sides –takes them to lunch or breakfast. Sharing a meal shows how someone interacts with service providers (like the wait staff), and how they treat those serving them is a very strong indication of their ability, and willingness, to be a leader. If someone isn't friendly and kind to those who are serving him, how will they treat someone who works for them? Pretty insightful if you ask me.

I have been able to weed out some 'professional interviewers' by having meals with candidates. I realize that this process can get expensive so it might not work in every organization or for every role, but people tend to let their guard down and be their true self over a meal and it can be a very revealing event.

I use this technique with some of my clients before accepting a big project.

Early in my time of business ownership when I was feeling the pressure to grow my customer base, I knew I needed to be strategic and selective, but I also needed to pay the bills. When I was asked to take on a fairly big consulting project for a mid-size property management company, I jumped on it.

I met with the owner and his management team and worked through all the details. I genuinely liked all of them and felt that I was a perfect fit for the scope of work they needed done.

Before the ink was fully dry on the contract, I regretted my decision.

The very day we signed, and they paid the deposit, the CEO wanted to take me around to visit the locations and meet the teams I'd be working with. We went to grab a quick bite first and that's where it happened.

He was incredibly rude and condescending to the hostess as we were being seated. And it just got worse when the waiter arrived at our table. This man clearly thought he was above being nice to the people who were going to be bringing his food, and he was obviously not worried about the spit – or something even grosser – that might end up on his sandwich.

It was an excruciatingly long lunch (that really only lasted about 40 minutes) and I spent the whole time wondering how I could get out of this situation.

You see, he had hired me because he felt like all of the 'good people' he hired didn't stay long. Who knew I'd be able to answer why forty minutes into what would normally be a fairly lengthy process??

There was surely more to the situation than just that one thing, but that one thing was HUGE! I mean, how do you think he treated the porters and groundskeepers at his properties? And it only took a few minutes at a few locations to realize that there was a huge amount of fear aimed toward the CEO. And the others on the management team were afraid of the CEO, too, and often used that fear to try to drive performance.

I'll spare you all the other details about that situation, but I will tell you this: it was the only time, as a business owner, I walked away from the contract. I had a frank conversation with the mean man who had hired me, told him I couldn't help his team until someone helped him.

And in order for someone to help him, he had to want the help. He didn't. And because he didn't want help, I couldn't help his organization because I was confident that he was the largest piece of the problem.

People who don't have the capacity to be kind to service providers and followers aren't bad leaders. They aren't leaders at all. Remember Chapter 2?

Assess First, Then Act

Whether you are new at leading, or just new to your current team, role, or organization, your approach has to reflect your newness.

There are sources out there that say up to 50% of new leaders fail to meet expectations in the first 18 months because of what they fail to do in the first 3 months. I can't speak to the statistical accuracy of that statement but based on my experience, it's spot on.

Many new leaders come into their new role like a tornado, shaking things up early on in an effort to prove their worth. It's like they feel they have to make a big mark in the first month to justify the choice the company made to hire them. And that's simply the worse thing a new leader can do.

If this is a promotion for you, you earned it because you're good at your job. Chances are, you've been working towards a promotion for a while.

Unfortunately, what often happens is we're so excited that we charge in like a bull chasing the red cape. That's a recipe for disaster. Your new role is not about you, or what you've accomplished. It's not about what you think you deserve, it's not a sign that you've paid your dues, and it's not a free ticket to do whatever you want. It's about the TEAM you are there to lead.

Newbie leaders must first gain the trust of their followers. Take time to learn how things are done now versus changing everything to 'your way' right off the bat. Taking your time to get to know the organization means you'll be able to focus on what's not working, versus spending time changing something that isn't broken.

I was working with an organization that just brought in a new division leader for their HR department. He came in and immediately swapped the company payroll to a different platform – the one he was used to from his old company, stating that the one currently being used was antiquated and wouldn't grow with the organization.

That may have been true, but what he didn't stop to consider is that the company had no plans for expansion in the near future until they fine-tuned some of their production processes. So, this guy – this newbie leader – came in and disrupted the whole payroll process in his first month on the job just so he'd know the system versus having to learn a new one.

He thought it would make him look like a hero – trying to make that early mark we mentioned earlier – but instead, he failed to plan for the glitches that always come with a system change like that and some of his front-line employees didn't get paid on time.

This guy's credibility went straight in the crapper, and he never really earned the trust of the team at all. A few months later, he moved on to his next adventure, just short of being asked to leave.

And it was a shame because he had the potential to be exactly what that organization needed IF he had just taken a moment to get to know the needs of the company and the team.

The lesson here is don't attempt to make drastic changes in hopes of making an immediate impact without taking time to learn the organization, the people, the culture, and the processes first. Not everything needs your stamp on it. And not everything needs to change to match 'your way'.

Not everything needs your stamp on it.

Your performance will be measured by how well your team performs. If your team fails, you fail. If they succeed, they get the credit. OK, you might get a little credit, but it really is all about the team.

Find a Mentor

Within the first few weeks in a new leader role, you'll want to find a mentor. You may already have one. If you do, you'll want to consider if that mentor is the one you need in your new position. Don't drop that mentor; just consider if you need an additional one.

Take the example of a friend of mine. She was the general manager of a restaurant; her mentor who was the general manager of a sister location. They were in the same position, but my friend's mentor had been in her GM role much longer, so she made an excellent choice as a mentor.

A few years later when the owner of those 2 restaurant locations bought 3 more locations, he needed someone to oversee all of them. My friend was promoted and now had to supervise the operations of 5 locations, including the location her mentor was running. She still respected her 'old' mentor but needed a new one – one who understood what she was up against now.

There may be someone in your organization that stands out as an obvious choice. Or someone in your professional circle that seems to fit the role.

Your supervisor might be an option but before settling on your boss as your mentor (or at least your only mentor), consider how things like your supervisor's accessibility, management style, schedule – in some cases, a supervisor, especially one with many direct reports spread over a large geographical area, may not have the time to mentor you the way you need.

And will you really be comfortable asking your boss questions while you are learning the intricacies of your new role? Probably not. Someone who is not in control of your paycheck is a better option.

Seek Feedback

Whether you're a newly promoted leader or just new to your current role or organization, you will need to seek out feedback. It's truly one of the only ways a good leader can become great.

You may be tired of hearing this already but it's not about you, it's about the people you serve as a leader. And if you are not meeting the needs of your followers, it doesn't really matter how good you are at anything. You will fail.

The best way to KNOW if you are meeting those needs is to **ask**.

Ask your peers. Ask your supervisor. ASK YOUR DIRECT REPORTS.

I bet I know what you're thinking. They won't answer you honestly because you're their boss and they don't want to risk their job. I understand why we worry about that.

But that's one of the reasons we have to establish trust early on. And why we need to create that environment of safety that we talked about earlier.

In the beginning, as you are working to get that 'safe place' culture established, you may have to rely on alternative ways to get feedback like engagement and culture surveys, 360 anonymous surveys, or even identifying someone on the front line that can act as the voice for the masses.

However you do it, you must do it. You simply MUST!

New leaders who go months, or worse, years, without asking for feedback almost never achieve sustained success. It's often far too late to right the ship by the time you figure out it's in a death roll and very few of your sailors will go down with you.

Here's a technique that may be helpful in getting feedback.

I would ask my team members this one question: what do I do that drives you crazy?

Everyone does something that gets on other peoples' nerves, even if we think we don't.

In the beginning when I'd ask that question, I'd get a lot of generic answers. 'Nothing that I can think of.' Or other similar non-committal answers.

But I decided I wasn't going to let them off the hook with a generic answer. I'd tell them, 'That's OK for now. But I'm going to ask you again in a week and I want a different answer.'

The next time I'd ask, in most cases, I'd get something useful.

One time in particular, when I was serving as VP of Operations, I asked the compliance manager on my team that question. And repeatedly, I'd get the standard 'nothing' answer. When I refused to accept that, she unloaded. ('Be careful what you wish' for came to mind that day!)

She told me that she hated how I red-lined everything policy and memo she sent to me for approval. My first thought was, 'that's my job!' But instead of making a knee-jerk response, I went back through some of the stuff of hers I had red-lined. And that was a real eye-opener!

I realized I hadn't just been red lining the very few grammatical errors or typos she made; I was changing her words to sound like they were mine. And all that red-lining I was doing was not only costing me valuable time, but it was also making her feel inadequate and frustrated.

Because I asked the question and made her answer it truthfully, I was able to adjust my approach to my red-lining and she felt more accomplished and appreciated. Win-win!

Another team member told me that it drove her crazy how I would leave sticky notes on her desk when she was away from her desk.

By doing what I thought was helpful – leaving little reminders and bits of info for her – I was really making her irritated. I didn't realize it until she pointed it out, but she didn't have one single sticky note on her desk except for mine. Turns out she hates sticky notes. She doesn't like how they sometimes stick to other things or get lost. She much preferred a neater approach.

She asked that I email her instead of leaving notes on her desk. Easy-peasy solution to what I didn't know was a problem until I asked!

Asking for feedback is only part of it.

You have to be willing to HEAR what you're told. There's an Arabian proverb that says:

"If one person calls you a donkey, get a second opinion. If two people call you a donkey, look in the mirror. If three people call you a donkey, get a saddle."

When we hear the feedback we get and pay attention to other cues, we can learn a lot about how other people perceive us. And their perception of you is their reality. If they perceive you to be sarcastic, it doesn't matter that you don't mean to be – the reality is they see you as sarcastic!

Listening to feedback also means you must take action sometimes. If I had listened to my team member complain about my red-lining process and done nothing about it, what would make her want to give me that type of feedback again?

CHAPTER 15:
LEADING AS A DECISION MAKER

Being a decision maker can be exciting. It can also be scary. What if you make the wrong decision? If it's a *small* bad decision, you can probably recover and do better next time. If it's a *big* bad decision, it might change the course of your future. And that makes it even scarier!

In most cases, by the time we reach a high level of decision-making autonomy, we have learned the art of good decision making, and better yet, learned how to deal with the not-so-good decisions we may make occasionally.

Unfortunately, when you are in a decision-maker's role, you will have to deal with all kinds of leadership challenges.

You'll have to deal with the apple polishers. You know, those people who behave fawningly towards someone they believe is important or have the power to benefit them in some way. You may use the term brown-noser or some other more colorful term. But in plain English, it's the people who will act subservient and agree with practically everything you say or do in order to stay in your good graces.

They may think that acting in such a way will make you like them, or that they'll be on the short list for perks or promotions. And in some cases, it's just in their nature to act that way towards someone they believe is in a role of power or control.

Whatever the case, you will deal with them in a decision-making role. You can bet on it!

You may think, 'I'll just ignore them.' But that would be a mistake.

Even if you could ignore them, many of their team members won't be able to. And the sycophant behavior is like acid on the floor of your ship. It can rot right through the hull of the team and cause big problems.

Apple polishing – or brown-nosing if you prefer – creates disdain, distrust, and out-and-out anger. And many of those team members who are tired of witnessing the polishing may also get tired of watching you ignore it. They may look to you to stop it, and when you don't, they may perceive that you like it and/or are heeding the BS that the polisher is throwing your way. Either way, it can damage your creditability, even though the behavior is completely generated by someone else.

You may want to start dealing with it by identifying what type of apple polisher you're dealing with. Many people who brown-nose are extremely insecure and are desperate for people to like them. Typically, this type of sycophant compliments and agrees with everyone, not just the decision maker. But the behavior can be amplified when dealing with those in power.

Others may use brown-nosing to camouflage their ineptitude at their job. They are constantly in self-preservation mode but may not be able or willing to actually change their performance to meet standards. They think it they get the boss to like them, the boss will be less likely to realize that they are poor performers.

Some of these folks simply believe that to 'suck up' to the decision makers is how to move up the ranks. They may think it's the best way to get noticed.

Rarely, the brown-noser is a top performer. The brown-nosing is often just a personality quirk that got out of hand. As the leader, this is one of the hardest challenges you'll face because you have to determine if the frustrating behavior is severe enough to risk crushing a superstar.

No matter the type of apple polisher you may have on the team – and the law of averages suggests that there will be at least one – you have to figure out what, if any, impact the behavior is having on the team, and how to deal with it so that the impact isn't long or far reaching, and so that you can preserve your leadership credibility.

CHAPTER 16: PERFORMANCE PUNISHMENT

At some point during your career, I'm betting you were the victim of performance punishment. Being good at your job attracts more work. You become sought out for difficult projects and important tasks because it has become evident that you can handle the pressure and do the work well.

When we first become the superstar at our job, it's flattering when we are given special projects or responsibilities that typically don't go with our role. It makes us feel important and we relish in knowing that others are taking note of our hard work.

After a while though, it becomes punishment - the more you do, the more they expect.

There are good chemicals your brain gets from being able to be the hero at work. If you are continually bailing out your manager or team, you've felt it. But before long, the good feeling you get from being needed turns sour. You may have liked getting those late afternoon/evening phone calls from team members who needed bailing out, but eventually, you'll realize that while you are fielding calls non-stop, a less competent coworker is able to relax at home in the evening because he's not having to bail anyone out.

And then, to quote neuroleadership.com:

That sweet brain candy is replaced by a fiery fight-or-flight response.

The article from neuroleadership.com goes on to say this: When the unfairness of the situation dawns on you, high performance turns into performance punishment and you start to resent being penalized with extra duties for being the better worker, and unequal assignments become unfair burdens.

Any form of performance punishment can breed resentment. If you haven't complained to your significant other or BFF about performance punishment at some point, you are the luckiest person in the business world.

I can remember my father complaining about it at the dinner table. And I remember Mom saying, 'just stop doing the extra work.' But we all know, it's not that simple. Once we've set the dangerous precedent of doing all that is asked of us, it's extremely hard to undo it.

I'm not going to talk about setting boundaries for ourselves. For some of us, it's too late anyway. We've worked past it. And it's more important to prevent it from happening to others.

Performance punishment – sometimes called quiet promoting – is a dangerous game. It puts us at risk of losing our top performers, because let's face it, they are the ones we keep dumping on over and over because we think they can take it.

All that dumping can cause burn out and feelings of being overwhelmed, and very few top performers will stick around long-term if they feel like they can't hold on to their superstardom without severe personal sacrifices.

I mean, this isn't one of those circumstances where you can chalk it up to everyone pays their dues. Punishment is not part of our dues. And we can't risk those superstars walking out the door because we don't want to prevent someone going through something yucky that we endured ourselves.

Performance punishment also puts us at risk of losing satisfactory performers who might turn into superstars one day. I mean, if we're giving all the extra work to the ones who are already top performers, how do we really know what those mid-level performers are capable of?

Come up with a plan. Map out what performance punishment looks like in your organization, note examples and situations from the past, and create a strategy with your team leaders, managers, and supervisors for preventing it from happening.

If you have employee surveys you send out, include a question on that survey about performance punishment. Are you doing stay interviews? (And if the answer is no, I'll give you a resounding, 'WHY NOT?') Add a question to your stay interviews about it. Talk about it. ASK the question.

CHAPTER 17:
OLIVE JUICE AND ELEPHANT SHOES

Olive Juice? When you mouth olive juice to someone across a room, it looks like you're saying I love you. Say it fast and it sounds like I love you. Elephant shoes is the same. You may remember that one from your childhood. And, right now, you're trying it! Go ahead. Give it a shot.

Olive juice.

Elephant Shoes.

I love you.

Pretty neat, right?

Well, I'm not really going to talk about olive juice or elephant shoes per se, but it got your attention, right?

What I want to talk about is saying *I love you* in the workplace.

Some of us don't want to use the L word too much, thinking that more frequent use might dilute the value. Others might use it too quickly. Many of us are afraid to use the L word in a professional environment. But there is no doubt that love is a powerful word and a powerful feeling.

I know, it sounds weird, but we need more olive juice and elephant shoes and LOVE in the workplace. And for most of my adult life, I thought that love only belonged in your personal life, and your personal life had to be kept strictly separate from your business life.

It's how I was raised. You checked your personal baggage at the door when you walked into work, and unless it was something truly extraordinary, personal stuff was never supposed to get in the way of living up to your work responsibilities.

And I still believe that concept applies to some degree in most situations. But I also believe that who we align ourselves with professionally is critically important. Not only do we need to work with an organization we trust and believe in, but one that has others there that have similar values and goals as your own.

When we surrounded ourselves with those that truly fit in our life, share our values and beliefs, and are working towards similar goals, it's perfectly OK to have some olive juice around! In fact, you SHOULD!!

My first exposure to olive juice – AKA I love you - in a professional environment:

A dozen or so years ago, I was serving on the board of directors of a trade association with some very professional leaders. That year, the president of the association lost his young daughter to a fatal disease. All of the directors stepped up to help him during that awful time, attending the service, reaching out with words and gifts of condolences, and picking up his duties as needed during his time of grief.

At the end of the president's term that year, he made the traditional 'thank you' speech at the last meeting he presided over as president. But his speech was different from every other one I had ever heard (and I had heard many!)

I really only remember one piece of it but it was a most profound piece.

He thanked everyone for their love and support during his family's tragedy and then he said, 'I love you all.'

Now, I already had a great deal of respect, and yes, love for this man. He was (and still is) a great leader, a gentle man and a gentleman, and a brilliant businessman. And to hear him say those words in a board meeting had a deep impact on me.

It was the first time I had allowed myself to think that it was OK in some situations to express love in a professional environment.

And it took some time to get used to that idea after so many years of believing that olive juice was a personal thing.

Once I got used to the concept, I started looking around my business environment, hoping to find olive juice. And I found some!

Now, I'm not saying that you should 'love' everyone in your workplace. Or that you should walk around saying I love you to everyone at work. That might turn weird quickly.

And we do have to think about what it would be like to tell a direct report you love her today, and then have to write her up tomorrow. That would be awkward beyond belief.

But I am saying this: the biggest blessing we can have in life is being around people we love and admire. And why must that be reserved for our personal lives?

I have been fortunate enough to work with people in every position I've held with whom I could share olive juice. But I'll admit that I've often forgotten to say it out l loud. I guess I have a little bit of fear that others will think it's weird.

Several times when I'd leave a position to move on to a new adventure, I'd tell some of those I was leaving behind that I loved them; some of them would tell me, too. And it felt good. It felt right.

Not too long ago, I was on the phone with a colleague that I've come to really care about, having a somewhat-emotional conversation about something that was really bothering her at her current job. When we got ready to hang up, I said, "I'll be thinking about you; I love you." With no hesitation, she sent olive juice right back over the phone line at me.

For a brief second, I thought 'that was weird.' But here's the thing – it wasn't. It was true, and natural, and needed to be said.

Tom Brady has won more Super Bowl® championships than any other player in NFL history.

There's no question he is a successful quarterback. But he's also an incredible leader. All you have to do is listen to how his teammates talk about him to know that.

And after his 2019 Super Bowl® win, we saw further evidence of his leadership. You may not have picked up on this as there was a lot of hoopla after the game, but Tom could be seen – and was caught on tape – using the same words over and over.

As he evaded several of the journalists who were clamoring to get an interview with the superstar QB, he went around hugging and congratulating other players. While he was running around embracing team members, he could be heard yelling, 'love you, man!' and 'I love you, dude!'

Now I know it was an exciting time for him and his team, having just won the BIG ONE. And emotions were high. But I believe that Tom exhibited two extremely valuable leadership competencies that day:

Vulnerability – I mean what makes you more vulnerable than shouting out 'I love you' on a football field amongst a bunch of 300 lb. brutes?

Authenticity – it was clear that the Tom that was running around saying I love you was the _real_ Tom, not some edited version of Tom Brady hyped up on adrenaline.

Note: Bill Murphy Jr., a contributing editor for Inc.com, has written several great articles about Tom Brady and his leadership if you want to read more about how he has achieved such great success. Sure, he's a great ball player but he's so much more than that!

Personally, I'm through with not telling the people that I love them. And I'm done with worrying about appropriateness and keeping personal stuff completely separate from my business relationships.

It's the realization that life is short, and to live a truly happy life, we need to surround ourselves with people we love. And we need to tell them we love them and not just assume they know.

Notice I said *we need to be around people we love*; not people that love us. Sure, most of the time those we love, love us back. But that's not the point. And in leadership, it's not about us – it's about them!

I'm sure there are some people that I love that may not love me back, and that's OK. Happiness comes from loving others; being loved back is just the icing on the cake.

Think about the people that you spend your time with at work. I bet there are some of them that you should be sharing olive juice with, too!

CHAPTER 18:
KEEPING THE SHIP AFLOAT
AND ON COURSE

Even though you are near the end of this book, and our time together for now, challenge yourself to continue your leadership growth journey!

Allow me to share a few final thoughts that may help on your continued journey.

Build Up Your Ship's Armament

As you witness leadership approaches that are effective and may be suitable for your leadership journey, add them to your **armament** closet. Arm yourself with every leadership tool possible. Keep a running list of books, blogs, TedTalks® and pod casts, quotes, resources, and anything else that may be helpful to you in your leadership journey.

And remind yourself everyday to CHOOSE leadership.

Use a Written Action Plan

You know it's true. When you write it down, you are more likely to DO IT. Write out your leadership action plan. Write it big and bold. Post it where you can see it. Show it to your family and peers. Show it to your direct reports. Sharing it with others will instill a higher self-accountability in your approach, and if you ask them, they will hold you accountable, too!

I write out my leadership action plan at the beginning of each quarter. That doesn't mean that I put NEW stuff on it each quarter. But the act of writing it down again helps keep it in the forefront of my mind, reminds me how many quarters I've been working on the same items, and makes me more determined to work harder on the items I have to repeatedly write down. And it reminds me to celebrate my progress!

Self-Reflection

Doing it each quarter also forces me to self-reflect frequently and prompts me to ask myself some questions. How am I doing with my goals? What could I be doing differently? What should I be doing that I'm not?

And not just those simple questions. Ask some hard ones, too. Here are a few suggestions:

- Does my leadership approach authentically represent my character and personality? Or are there components of the approach I am attempting that stretch past my core character?

- Am I aligned with the right organization and people? Am I allowed to be the leader I want to be where I am?

- Am I trying hard enough to be the leader I want to be? Or are there large periods of time where I 'forget' my leadership goals?

- Am I allowing others to lead? Am I able to follow?

- Have I seen leadership growth in my team recently?
  - YES? Did I celebrate that growth with them? Am I nurturing that growth?
  - NO? What should I be doing to help them grow their leadership skills?

Give Yourself a Break!

Rome wasn't built in a day, and neither is a great leader! Be realistic in your expectations of yourself and your leadership growth. It takes time to change your approach, to break habits and create new ones, and to adapt to a new situation or environment.

Whether you are on a new journey, or charting a new course for an existing journey, give yourself a break. You will misstep. It's OK. The important part is to keep going. And celebrate each little victory along the way!